SCJ-HNS

HON'BLE SUPREME COURT OF INDIA

FCS NAVEEN BHATNAGAR

ISBN 978-1-63832-890-2

My Beloved Parents (Late) Er. K.P. Bhatnagar & Savita Bhatnagar are a constant inspiration. All my works are dedicated to their Lotus Feet.

Contents

FOREWORD

FCS Naveen Bhatnagar
    Celebrated Author Globally

OM Sai Ram... Friends, Readers, Dear Students, NBR Today is Your Friend Next-Door.

Blessed to be Mentored by IIM Founders; Govt/Political dispensation and more. Privileged to have Advised Leading Film, Sports Celebrities World-over. From Mahi, Choti Sardarni, Neil John Taylor, Craig Mc Dermott....never ending company, ever-since childhood.

Strong acumen to learning, mentoring helped me make 'SMILE' with a purpose. Equally, blessed over 1,000 Lovely Students in Multi-faceted areas such as Law, Economics, Costing, Accountancy, Financial Management. My Authored Book's (presently 17 Book's, increasing @ 15 Days) seeks your overwhelming support, blessing. **In 07 Hrs Master any Subject.**

Preface

NBR Today® provides Bare Act/s, Subject/s of interest for Professionals; Students pursuing Competitive Exams, Professional Courses in form of Ready Reckoner/ Digest/ Guide. NBR Today® is focussed to enhance, support common man's Knowledge, Understanding & gained reasonable recognition amongst Students, Academicians, Professional's, Government. It is easy to read, understand & grasp & for those matters connected therewith or incidental thereto.

Please note with caution that no work is complete, unless supplemented with practice, books, notes, guidance from Teachers, Elders & above all – Parents Love & Respect.

All possible precaution & care has been taken in this material to avoid mistakes & omissions etc. for which the Author/Editor, publisher and /or the sellers are not in any way responsible. All disputes are subject to Delhi Courts. Maximum liability is limited to return amount paid by concerned purchaser/ reader.

Acknowledgements

Author acknowledges invaluable contribution of his **Wife & Daughter** who took considerable pains in the development & review of the title, manuscript. Also, professional colleagues, relatives who took pains & reworked & updated this material to meet, suit requirement of the Reader's.

We will be failing in our duty if we do not acknowledge the contribution of *Amazon, Flipkart, Notion Press, etc.* who helped in publishing & in bringing out this material, publication.

In end, each one of our students is a precious 'Gem' – generation next, entering the new arena, aspiring to seek higher education, especially as professionals, opening new frontiers, all this to unravel "Excellence" as they move up in the higher echelons as Academician, Corporate Ladder, successful Entrepreneur, Home-makers. For sure, your rich idea's, honest feedback will certainly help improve, enrich to serve in a better way.

PROLOGUE

NBR Today® is focussed to enhance, support common man's Legal Knowledge, Understanding & gained reasonable recognition amongst Students, Academicians, Professional's, Government. A number of Voluminous yet Complex Laws affect every Indian's daily chores, which are avidly considered & addressed/answered in NBR Today®. Untiring Journey towards Excellence in the field of Law is what least I get inspired & NBR Today® is one such effort. I continue to do a lot of work for Professional enrichment & Prime importance.

I

Hon'ble Supreme Court of India decided cases Head Notes & Synopsis

DOJ: 09.01.2019
NBR (2019) (01) (01) (01)
IN THE SUPREME COURT OF INDIA
CIVIL APPELLATE JURISDICTION
REGIONAL TRANSPORT OFFICER & ORS. ETC.................APPELLANT(S)
VERSUS
K. JAYACHANDRA & ANR. ETC...................................RESPONDENT(S)
CIVIL APPEAL NOS. 219 - 222 OF 2019
(ARISING OUT OF S.L.P. (C) NOS.13228 - 13231 OF 2013)
With C.A. No. 223 of 2019 [@ SLP [C] No. 27499 / 2013]

Arun Mishra and Vineet Saran, JJ.

CASES CITED

1. Avishek Goenka (1) v. Union of India & Anr. (2012) 5 SCC 321 [Para 20]

2. R. Ramasamy v. The Secretary, Ministry of Transport, Chennai & Ors. (2009) 1 Mad. LJ 1027 [Para 22]

3. K.S. Rajesh Kumar v. The Additional Registering Authority of Kerala High Court [Para. 24]

4. Mohd. Javeed v. Union of India & Ors. (2001) 9 ALD 88 = 2009 1 ALT 507 [Para. 25]

5. V.N. Dharmakrishnan v. Deputy Commissioner of Transport, AIR 2006 Mad. 340 [Para. 26]

HEAD NOTE

Alteration - against Motor Vehicles Act, 1988 ("Act") norms which indented *public safety* - except section 52 prohibitions, as per Rules State notifications permitted owners of 10 or more transport vehicles to alter, without approval, but to report within 14 days - Amendment Act, 2000 eased prohibition for Liquefied Petroleum Gas (LPG) eco-friendly vehicles and Central Government specified purposes – alter particulars in registration certificate without changing original manufacturer's specification - earlier, Kerala Transport Commissioner's Circular No.7/2006 denied registration where Vehicle body violate original manufacturer specification - section 52 and Rules not correctly interpreted by Division Bench, Kerala High Court - impugned judgment suggesting no total prohibition to alter set aside. [paras 7,12,17, 23, 33]

Appeals allowed.

SYNOPSIS

Alter Motor Vehicle - section 52 of the Motor Vehicles Act, 1988 ("Act"), Rule 126 of Central Motor Vehicles Rules, 1989 [central rules] and the effect of Rules 96, 103 and 261 of the Kerala Motor Vehicle Rules, 1989 [state rules] - Transport Commissioner, Kerala Circular No.7/2006 body of vehicle in violation manufacturer specifications denied registration - conflict in judgments in Writ Petitions whether alteration is permissible - Division Bench of High Court structural alteration is permissible as per state Rules – Section 52 amend that alteration certificate of registration in variance originally specified by manufacturer, owner makes modification engine - Central Government may prescribe specifications conditions - State Government notifications to permit owning not less than ten transport vehicles to alter any vehicle owned, without the approval of registering authority - within 14 days alteration, report jurisdiction authority - Rule 126 of the Central Rules prototype of every motor vehicle subject to test - base model less than 250 in any consecutive period of six months in a year, then such base model and its variants need not be subjected to test, if at least one model subjected to such tests at least once in a year - Rule 93 deals overall dimension - Rules 96, 103 and 261 of Kerala Rules, 1989, provide for inspection, recording alteration and body construction - Division Bench, High Court in the impugned judgment has opined that alteration not totally prohibited - urged section 52 of the Act and Rule 126, as well as the Kerala

Rules, have not been correctly interpreted by the High Court - It is not permissible to Rules in contravention section 52 - not permissible to alter the vehicle in derogation to the provisions of the Act- legislative intent "public safety" of the Act - interpretation Rules serve legislative intent - neither be permissible nor possible for the Court to read into these statutory provisions, what is not specifically provided for- object of framing such rules, in preference to one which would frustrate, must give larger public interest - Section 52(2) of the New Act which related to deemed approval on expiry of seven days has also been deleted - Under Section 52(4) of New Act, owner report alteration with the approval or deemed approval- word "registration" in the Amended Act mistake, instead "alteration" - intended alteration made be incorporated in the Registration Certificate (RC) - comparison Old and New Act with Amendment Act dispensed permission for change or modification effected in a motor vehicle – Madras High Court held alternation not permissible in variance with RC, not result basic feature change, consider section 52 of Amended Act - *V.N. Dharmakrishnan v. Deputy Commissioner of Transport*, AIR 2006 Mad. 340 relied - Delivery Van Goods Carrier can be altered as an ambulance - held clear violation - cannot be condoned ground render free service - 52(1) permits modification - empowers the Central Government to prescribe specifications, conditions for approval, retrofitment and other related - Section 52(2) State Government permit owning atleast 10 transport vehicles replace 'engine' same make and type, without approval - Where no approval, Section 52(3) alteration owner report within 14 days - Rule 92(1) read as subservient to section 52 once entered in certificate of registration, cannot be varied - Central Rules, prototype subject to test - alteration under the Rules is permissible except as prohibited by section 52 - not to vary original specifications by manufacturer - Remaining particulars in RC can be modified - As such, the decision rendered by the Division Bench cannot be said to be laying down the law correctly - Rules are subservient to Act and COR changed except, specifications manufacturer - Circular No.7/2006 read in that spirit - impugned judgment set aside - appeals allowed.

DOJ: 14.01.2019
NBR 2019 (1) (2) (2)
IN THE SUPREME COURT OF INDIA
CRIMINAL APPELLATE JURISDICTION
CRIMINAL APPEAL NO 1980 OF 2008

Ashish Jain ...Appellant
Versus
Makrand Singh and Ors. ...Respondents
With
CRIMINAL APPEAL NO 1981 OF 2008
State of Madhya Pradesh ...Appellant
Versus
Makrand Singh and Ors. ...Respondents

CASES CITED

- *Selvi* v. *State of Karnataka*, (2010) 7 SCC 263
- *Mohd. Aman* v. *State of Rajasthan*, (1997) 10 SCC 44
- *State of Rajasthan* v. *Islam and Ors.*, (2011) 6 SCC 343
- *State of U.P.* v. *Awdhesh*, (2008) 16 SCC 238
- *State (Delhi Admin.)* v. *Laxman Kumar and Ors.*, (1985) 4 SCC 476
- *Sonvir* v. *State (NCT) of Delhi*, (2018) 8 SCC 24
- *Shankaria* v. *State of Rajasthan*, (1978) 3 SCC 435

HEAD NOTE

Appeal – Death reference - establish *inter-se relation* under Cr PC between Section 27 Evidence Act on 'theory of confirmation by subsequent facts' & Article 20 (3) of Constitution on 'Right against self incrimination' - first circumstance relied by prosecution is *last seen circumstance*, not proved nor establish weapons used - supported other circumstantial evidence on *'last seen evidence'* & *'stolen property recovered'* – sections 34, 302, 394, 449 IPC., 11, 13 of M.P. Dakaiti & Vyapharan Prabhavit Kshetra Adhiniyam (MPDVPKA); offences u/s 25(1) (b) (a), 27 of Arms Act - none of the respondents appeared before SC - SC appoint *amicus curiaes* to argue - murder, robbery in house on electrical repairs pretext - After FIR investigation, Executive Magistrate identified, all 03 accused/s confessed – DIG Police visit inferred crime - investigation & prosecution concocted - accused/s not abscond, unnatural - recovery on involuntary confession inadmissible & identification improper - nothing to show pledgors identity - fingerprints illegal - two left witnesses statement afterthought – wrongly found guilty by Trial Court - appellant/ nephew of deceased & State failed to establish HC erred - SC upheld HC judgment & order – acquittal of accused confirmed.[paras 1, 3, 16, 20, 21, 23, 28, 29]....Appeals dismissed.

SYNOPSIS

Appeal- High Court of Madhya Pradesh in Death Reference - impugned judgments acquitted accused – Sections 302 read with 34, 394 read with 34 and 449 of the Indian Penal Code and Sections 11 read with 13 of the Madhya Pradesh Dakaiti and Vyapharan Prabhavit Kshetra Adhiniyam (in short "the MPDVPKA") for offences under Section 25(1)(b)(a) read with Section 27 of Arms Act and Sections 11 and 13 of the MPDVPKA – death of three people and robbery - pretext of electrical repairs entered house and committed murder and robbery - locked the house from outside and fled – appellant, nephew of deceased asked some relatives whereabouts, no avail - informed the Police Station- broke open - lying dead third floor - Multiple injuries - chest used gold, ornaments and cash broken open with its contents missing – electricians, regular repair works committed offence – FIR by nephew - after investigation accused persons arrested next morning - robbed gold, ornaments, cash, bloodstained clothes, and certain electrical tools, weapons, keys recovered - robbed ornaments were pledged by different people - naib Tehsildar, Executive Magistrate, conducted identification - Trial Court, charges and evidence, found guilty and sentenced - revolves around Ashish Jain statements, complainant - Kailash Chandra, brother of deceased neighboring shopkeeper as well as a relative, had told him seen accused entering the house around 6:00 6: 30 p.m. the previous evening carrying a bag containing electrical equipment - Vinod Kumar Jain seen the accused persons coming out between 9:00 9: 30 p.m. going towards Dharamshala in hurried fashion with 2 bags - first circumstance relied upon by prosecution is "last seen circumstance" - K.D. Sonakiya, I.O. deposed as witness before Trial Court - present at scene of incident from start and completed investigation - incriminating circumstance against accused - recovery of various articles based on their statements - All confessed committing the crime and recovery - country made pistol seized Other incriminating material seized - postmortem report examined by Trial Court - lacerated wounds - all injuries were ante-mortem sufficient to cause death - cause of death 'shock' due to haemorrhage - appellant opposed acquittal - articles sufficient ground for conviction, further supported by other circumstantial evidence - hair sample test report inconclusive - State of Madhya Pradesh filed appeal against acquittal by High Court- circumstantial evidence fully proved lead to conviction - Supreme Court Legal Services Committee was directed engage counsel for the accused Respondents since none had appeared for them - Amicus Curiae was appointed - supported majority view taken by High Court in acquitting - argued discrepancies in evidence - stated only one witness examined – non-examination of other key witnesses be crucial for prosecution - no proper procedure followed for identification of ornaments - interest in the identification of ornaments - last seen circumstance not proved - present case of circumstantial evidence primarily hinges on two main aspects, which is the last seen evidence and the recovery of stolen property - deliberate delay in recording statements of important witnesses with regard to the last seen circumstance - statements of witnesses afterthought - chance witness with material discrepancies - inclined to discard his evidence as last seen circumstance - accused persons were not absconding, which is unnatural - recovery of the incriminating material caused by inducement, pressure or coercion - confessional statement involuntary, hit by Article 20(3) of the Constitution, inadmissible - statement under undue pressure evidentiary value is nullified - observations of this Court regarding the relationship between Section 27 of the Evidence Act and Article 20(3) of the Constitution in *Selvi* v. *State of Karnataka,* (2010) 7 SCC 263 - right against self incrimination viewed as an essential safeguard in criminal procedure - two objectives firstly, ensuring statement reliability and secondly made voluntarily - serves as a check on police behaviour during investigation - useful to refer to Sections 162, 163 and 164 Cr PC which lay down procedural safeguards in respect of statements during investigation - Section 27 of Evidence Act incorporates theory of confirmation by subsequent facts - any fact is deposed to as discovered in consequence of information received from a person accused of any offence, in the custody of a police officer, so much of such information, whether it amounts to a confession or not, as relates distinctly to the fact thereby discovered, may be proved." - there is no automatic presumption that the custodial statements have been extracted through compulsion - person was indeed compelled to make statements while in custody, relying on such testimony as well as its derivative use will offend Article 20(3) - relationship between Section 27 of the Evidence Act and Article 20(3) of the Constitution was clarified in *Kathi Kalu Oghad* [AIR 1961 SC 1808 : (1961) 2 Cri LJ 856 : (1962) 3 SCR 10 - self-incriminatory information without any threat- not hit by Article 20(3) of Constitution - It must, therefore, be held that the provisions of Section 27 of the Evidence Act are not within the prohibition aforesaid, unless compulsion used in obtaining the information - recovered stolen ornaments, etc basis of involuntary statements- negates incriminating circumstance severely undermines prosecution case - identification not done in due procedure - nothing to show identity of pledgors and to prove identified ornaments were pledged by them to the deceased Premchand - none of witnesses spoken about particular entry relating to them in account books - artificial and gotup story in identification – non examination of two important witnesses affects prosecution case - prosecution not established weapons used for crime - All the bloodstained items sent to FSL examination, however reports not help prosecution - fingerprints of Accused illegally obtained without magisterial order - *Mohd. Aman* v. *State of Rajasthan*, (1997) 10 SCC 44 prosecution has failed to establish that the seized articles were not or could not be tampered with before it reached the Bureau for examination. Further the following was stated in para 8: (*Mohd. Aman case* [*Mohd.Aman* v. *State of Rajasthan*, (1997) 10 SCC 44 : 1997 SCC (Cri) 777] , SCC p. 49) specimen fingerprints of Mohd. Aman had to be taken on a number of occasions at the behest of the Bureau, they were never taken before or under the order of a Magistrate in accordance with Section 5 of the Identification of Prisoners Act - It is noteworthy to mention that the DIG of Police had visited the scene of the crime - inferred crime by 3 electricians- whole investigation and prosecution concocted around - well reasonably accept High Court view - appellants failed to establish High Court erred in conclusion - blatant illegality or substantial error in acquittal proved appellants, this Court not interfere - As a reasonable suspicion or doubt persists in our minds regarding the guilt of the accused based on the case of the prosecution, the scales of criminal justice tilt in favour of acquittal of the accused. In such a scenario, acquittal of accused confirmed - Criminal Appeal dismissed - judgment and order of acquittal by High Court maintained.

DOJ: 25.01.2019
NBR (2019) (01) (02) (01)
IN THE SUPREME COURT OF INDIA
CRIMINAL ORIGINAL JURISDICTION
WRIT PETITION (Crl.) No.142 OF 2018
Ramesh Sanka ....Petitioner (s)
VERSUS
Union of India & Ors. ....Respondent(s)
ABHAY MANOHAR SAPRE AND R. SUBHASH REDDY...JJ
CASES CITED

- State of Uttaranchal vs. Balwant Singh Chaufal & Ors. [2010(3) SCC 402] [Para. 15]
- K.D. Sharma vs. Steel Authority of India Ltd. & Ors. [2008(12) SCC 481 [Para. 15]
- Arun Kumar Agrawal vs. Union of India & Ors. [2014(2) SCC 609] [Para. 15]

HEAD NOTE

Mandamus dismissed seeking CBI investigation - no merit under Article 32 for personal contractual rights, also, no relief sought in person – held, no Fundamental Rights violated - no Relief as per law laid in earlier cases – Petitioner, ex-CEO pleading Respondent Company {'R'} committed several cognizable financial irregularities - R *suo motu* appeared, filed status report – explore other Civil remedy, adjudication before appropriate Judicial Forum - for other grievances, SC issues Notice to other respondents – appropriate action those found guilty – not expressed opinion on several issues which will not influence other ongoing proceedings [paras 1, 6, 11,16,17,20]... Writ Dismissed.

SYNOPSIS

Article 32 - Writ of Mandamus - CBI to investigate - Petitioner, former employee of Limited Company worked as CEO - grievance - *modus operandi* of Respondent No.12 Company- carrying out their business and financial operations/dealings - persons who are managing its affairs - also against the Companies, individuals and the firms with whom they are having business and financial dealing/operations - committed several financial irregularities - having work places in contravention of Several Acts / Rules - all such dealings/activities caused heavy loss to public exchequer but also liable for several cognizable offences punishable - On 11.07.2018, this Court issued notice of this writ petition confining it to the official respondents namely, respondent Nos.7 to 11 - These respondents have filed the status report in a sealed cover - One official respondent has filed the affidavit - Respondent No.12 – Company, however, in the meantime entered *suo motu* appearance and has filed IA praying therein for dismissal of the writ petition on legal as well as on factual grounds - writ deserves dismissal - not a *bona fide* petition – writ filed with ulterior motive - tarnish image in the market - writ not involve violation of fundamental right - writ petitioner has countered the averments made in the aforesaid IA by placing reliance on the averments made in the writ petition contending that there has been no suppression of the material facts as alleged by respondent No.12 – Company - heard - law laid down by this Court in few other cases, not inclined grant any relief - not claimed any relief in person - Even otherwise, no writ at instance of any employee or the employer for claiming enforcement of any personal contractual rights *inter se* It is not in dispute their grievances - Civil Court be pursued in accordance with law against each other - So far as the raising of other grievances as set out *supra* by the writ petitioner against the other respondents are concerned, suffice it to say, this court by order dated 11.07.2018 had issued notice to the official respondents Nos.7 to 11 - respondents filed respective status report in relation to the inquiries - perused - appropriate action as provided in law will follow against all those who are found guilty -Before parting, we make it clear that we have not expressed any opinion on several factual issues alleged and denied by all the parties against each other in this writ petition and in respective IAs - This order, therefore, will not influence any authority or the Court or ongoing inquiry or proceedings while dealing with any issue. The same has to be dealt with uninfluenced by this order- not necessary several IAs - all such applicants raise their grievances *qua* respondent No.12 - remedy lies in filing Civil Suit - Company whether individually or severally for adjudication of their rights before an appropriate Judicial Forum in accordance with law- no merit in this writ petition - dismissed.

DOJ: 25.01.2019
NBR 2019(1) (7) (1)
IN THE SUPREME COURT OF INDIA
CIVIL ORIGINAL/APPELLATE JURISDICTION
WRIT PETITION (CIVIL) NO. 99 OF 2018
Swiss Ribbons Pvt. Ltd. & Anr .....Petitioners
VERSUS
Union of India & Ors . ...Respondents
WITH
WRIT PETITION (CIVIL) NO. 100 OF 2018
WRIT PETITION (CIVIL) NO. 115 OF 2018
WRIT PETITION (CIVIL) NO. 459 OF 2018
WRIT PETITION (CIVIL) NO. 598 OF 2018
WRIT PETITION (CIVIL) NO. 775 OF 2018
WRIT PETITION (CIVIL) NO. 822 OF 2018
WRIT PETITION (CIVIL) NO. 849 OF 2018

WRIT PETITION (CIVIL) NO. 1221 OF 2018
SPECIAL LEAVE PETITION (CIVIL) NO. 28623 OF 2018
WRIT PETITION (CIVIL) NO. 37 OF 2019

R.F. Nariman and Navin Sinha ....JJ.

<u>CASES REFERRED</u>

- Madras Bar Association v. Union of India (2015) 8 SCC 583
- Uttara Foods & Feeds Pvt. Ltd. v. Mona Pharmachem, Civil Appeal No. 18520/2017
- Arcelor Mittal India Private Limited v. Satish Kumar Gupta & Ors., Civil Appeal Nos. 9402-9405/2018
- Brilliant Alloys Pvt. Ltd. v. Mr. S. Rajagopal & Ors., SLP (Civil) No. 31557/ 2018
- State Bank's Staff Union (Madras Circle) v. Union of India & Ors., (2005) 7 SCC 584
- Shayara Bano v. Union of India, (2017) 9 SCC 1
- Union of India v. R. Gandhi, President, Madras Bar Association (2010) 11 SCC 1
- Madras Petrochem Ltd. and Anr. v. Board for Industrial and Financial Reconstruction and Ors., (2016) 4 SCC 1
- Innoventive Industries Ltd. v. ICICI Bank and Anr., (2018) 1 SCC 407
- R.K. Garg v. Union of India, (1981) 4 SCC 675
- DG of Foreign Trade v. Kanak Exports, (2016) 2 SCC 226
- Balco Employees' Union v. Union of India, (2002) 2 SCC 333
- S.P. Sampath Kumar v. Union of India, (1987) 1 SCC 124 : (1987) 2 ATC 82
- L. Chandra Kumar v. Union of India, (1997) 3 SCC 261 : 1997 SCC (L&S) 577
- Delhi International Airport Limited v. International Lease Finance Corporation and Ors., (2015) 8 SCC 446
- Natural Resources Allocation, In re, Special Reference No. 1 of 2012, (2012) 10 SCC 1
- State of A.P. v. McDowell and Co., (1996) 3 SCC 709
- Ajay Hasia v. Khalid Mujib Sehravardi, (1981) 1 SCC 722 : 1981 SCC (L&S) 258
- Subramanian Swamy v. CBI, (2014) 8 SCC 682: (2014) 6 SCC (Cri) 42: (2014) 3 SCC (L&S) 36
- Gopal Jha v. The Hon'ble Supreme Court of India, Writ Petition (Civil) No. 745/2018

- Indian Young Lawyers Associations and Ors. v. State of Kerala and Ors., Writ Petition (Civil) No. 373/2006
- Joseph Shine v. Union of India, Writ Petition (Criminal) No. 194/2017
- K.S. Puttaswamy v. Union of India, Writ Petition (Civil) No. 494/2012
- Navtej Singh Johar and Ors. v. Union of India, (2018) 10 SCC 1
- Lok Prahari v. State of Uttar Pradesh and Ors., (2018) 6 SCC 1
- Nikesh Tarachand Shah v. Union of India and Ors., (2018) 11 SCC 1
- Construction Pvt. Ltd. v. Ninus Finance & Investment Lokhandwala Kataria Manager LLP, Civil Appeal No. 9279 of 2017;
- Mothers Pride Dairy India Private Limited v. Portrait Advertising and Marketing Private Limited, Civil Appeal No. 9286/2017;
- Uttara Foods and Feeds Private Limited v. Mona Pharmacem, Civil Appeal No. 18520/2017]
- Salomon v. A Salomon and Co. Ltd. [1897] AC 22
- State Bank's Staff Union (Madras Circle) v. Union of India and Ors., (2005) 7 SCC 584
- Ritesh Agarwal and Anr. v. SEBI and Ors., (2008) 8 SCC 205
- K.S. Paripoornan v. State of Kerala and Ors., (1994) 5 SCC 593
- Darshan Singh v. Ram Pal Singh and Anr., 1992 Supp (1) SCC 191
- Pyare Lal Sharma v. Managing Director and Ors., (1989) 3 SCC 448
- P.D. Aggarwal and Ors. v. State of U.P. and Ors., (1987) 3 SCC 622
- Govind Das and Ors. v. Income Tax Officer and Anr., (1976) 1 SCC 906
- Attorney General for India and Ors. v. Amratlal Prajivandas and Ors., (1994) 5 SCC 54.

HEAD NOTE

IBC CONSTITUTIONAL VALIDITY – members appointment improper - upon SC direction SelC constituted and to constitute Circuit Benches in 6 months - fourfold attack on S.29A(c), countered including maximize stressed assets value and liquidation is last resort – moved from inability to pay debts to determine default - operational creditors not discriminated under Article 14 - u/s 60 COC not have last word, NCLT/NCLAT can set aside - these reasons, S.12A passes constitutional muster - PRIVATE IU INFORMATION - take authentication & verification – records evidence of default only - RP NO ADJUDICATION POWERS – AA only vet & verify claims - make determination under R.35A apply to AA for relief - settled this statute is not retrospective - S.29A (C) NOT RESTRICTED TO MALFEASANCE - S.35(1)(f) proviso added retrospective is arbitrary & violates Article 14 of

Constitution.- ONE YEAR PERIOD IN S. 29A(C) & NPA - eligibility to submit RPL - willful defaulter - NPA, declared as such under RBI guidelines - ineligibility after one year as NPA is doubtful asset - RELATED PARTY - constitutional challenge against S.29A (j) definition - MSME EXEMPTED FROM S.29A - SME form foundation of economy - SECTION 53 NOT VIOLATE ARTICLE 14 - IBC deals economic matters – its working monitored - defaulter's paradise lost - all petitions be disposed as per this judgment [paras 2, 4,16, 19,25, 36,48, 53, 62,64, 68, 72,77, 79,85, 86]...NO ORDER AS TO COSTS.

<u>SYNOPSIS</u>

IBC Constitutional validity - NCLT, NCLAT members appointment against SC judgment in Madras Bar Association v. Union of India (2015) 8 SCC 583 - operational creditors discriminated - unless 10% of aggregate debt owed, no voice in COC for financial creditors; operational creditors no vote – IU certification, sole object is profit – S.12A contrary to SC order in Uttara Foods & Feeds Pvt. Ltd. v. Mona Pharmachem, Civil Appeal No. 18520/ 2017 - RP adjudication being non-judicial authority violate dispensation of justice - fourfold attack on S.29A(c) i.e. erstwhile promoters participate in recovery; impair maximization of assets value; NPA by RBI, despite not 'willful' defaulter; 1 year arbitrary and related parties debarred - Govt. counsels countered that previous legislation failed to maximize stressed assets value - focused corporate debtor revival - creditors differentiation on contract nature - financial creditors better equipped - fallacy no notice on defaults to financial debtor, fully aware - S.12A creditor application admitted is proceeding in rem - 90% creditors given task to halt as proceeding in rem - in Arcelor Mittal India Private Limited v. Satish Kumar Gupta & Ors., Civil Appeal Nos. 9402-9405/2018 held S.29A not retrospective - one year is sufficient, declared as sub-standard asset – liquidation last resort – focus on revival.

<u>NCLT & NCLAT MEMBERS APPOINT NOT VIOLATE</u>- RD, MCA Affidavit – upon SC directed SelC constituted - Circuit Benches in 6 months hereof – rectify MCA administrative support – held no discriminate financial, secured & operational, unsecured creditors – information easily available through IU under IUR to financial creditors and wrongly invoke S.7 punish – u/s 60 before AA challengeable - counterclaims preserved for admission stage - move away from inability to pay debts to determine default - four policy reasons in shift i.e. predictability & certainty; corporate debtor paramount interest & admission into IRP not prejudice but protects; cause

of default is not relevant in financial stress and to protect corporate debtor economic interest - trigger lead to liquidation on RPL failure - RPL cannot pass unless minimum payment to operational creditors made, not less than liquidation value with priority over financial creditors - not discriminated under Article 14 - Brilliant Alloys Pvt. Ltd. v. Mr. S. Rajagopal & Ors., SLP (Civil) No. 31557/2018 withdrawal application in exception - once IBC triggered by admission of a creditor's petition u/s 7 to 9, AA proceeding in rem - necessary body oversee RP be consulted before any settle - any stage COC not constituted, approach NCLT - thrust against S.12A is 90% COC allow withdrawal – u/s 60 COC not have last word, NCLT/NCLAT can set aside - these reasons, S.12A passes constitutional muster.

<u>PRIVATE IU INFORMATION ONLY PRIMA FACIE EVIDENCE OF DEFAULT</u>- not governed properly- IUR undertake authentication & verification, communicate to all – records only prima facie evidence of default.

<u>RP NO ADJUDICATION POWERS</u>– only vet & verify claims - administrative powers - make "determination" under R. 35A apply to AA for relief - cannot act without COC approval.

<u>RETROSPECTIVE APPLICATION</u>- settled statute is not retrospective - State Bank's Staff Union (Madras Circle) v. Union of India & Ors., (2005) 7 SCC 584 - RA no vested right for RPL approval - right taken away by S.29A.

<u>SECTION 29A (C) NOT RESTRICTED TO MALFEASANCE</u> - person need not be a criminal for keeping outside RPL - proviso to Section 35(1)(f) added retrospective is arbitrary & violates Article 14 of Constitution.

<u>ONE-YEAR PERIOD IN S. 29A(C) & NPA</u>- eligibility to submit RPL - willful defaulter - NPA, declared as such under RBI guidelines – RBI's Master Circular instructions on NPAs - declared NPA only if defaults not resolved for more than 90 days in term loan, be NPA for 12 months unable to service its own debt beyond grace period is unfit be RA - ineligibility after one year as NPA is doubtful asset.

<u>RELATED PARTY</u> - constitutional challenge against S.29A(j) with "related party" definition - persons u/s 5(24A) be "connected" with RA.

<u>EXEMPTION OF MSME FROM S.29A</u> - SME form foundation of economy - exempted these industries - other resolution applicants not be forthcoming but liquidation – S.240A, retrospective effect.

<u>SECTION 53 NOT VIOLATE ARTICLE 14</u>- IBC deals economic matters, largely country's economy - working of IBC monitored - financial resource to commercial sector in India increased, result of financial debts being

repaid - 3300 cases in out-of-court settlements claims over INR 1,20,390 crores - 80 cases resolution plans accepted of INR 60,000 crores, over 202% of liquidation value - total flow of resources to commercial sector increased - IBC proving successful - defaulter's paradise lost - all petitions be disposed as per this judgment - no order as to costs.

ABBREVIATIONS

Acts

IBC - Insolvency & Bankruptcy Code, 2016

Department/s

MCA - Ministry of Corporate Affairs

RD - Regional Director

UOI – Union of India

Courts/ Tribunals

SC - Supreme Court

NCLAT – National Company Law Appellate Tribunal

NCLT – National Company Law Tribunal

Others

AA - Adjudicating Authority

COC – committee of Creditors

CIC- Credit Information Company

CD- Corporate Debtor

CIRP - Corporate Insolvency Resolution Process

EOI – Expression of Interest

NPA - Non Performing Asset

RA - Resolution Applicant

RP - Resolution Professional

RPL - Resolution Plan

S. – Section

SelC - Selection Committee

IRP – Insolvency Resolution Professional

IU – Information Utilities

IUR - IBBI India (Information Utilities) Regulations, 2017

DOJ: 20.02.2019

NBR 2019 (02) (10) (01)

IN THE SUPREME COURT OF INDIA

CIVIL APPELLATE JURISDICTION

SPECIAL LEAVE PETITION (CIVIL) NO. 540 OF 2018

LMJ International Ltd. .....Petitioner(s)
Versus
Sleepwell Industries Co. Ltd. ....Respondent(s)
WITH
SPECIAL LEAVE PETITION (CIVIL) NO. 5493 OF 2019
(D. No.42537/2018)
Sri Munisuvrata Agri International Ltd. .....Petitioner(s)
Versus
Sleepwell Industries Co. Ltd. ....Respondent(s)

A.M. Khanwilkar & Ajay Rastogi ....JJ

Cases referred:

a. *Shri Lal Mahal Ltd. Vs. Progetto Grano SPA1*
b. *Renusagar Power Company Ltd. Vs. General Electric Co.2*
c. *Oil & Natural Gas Corporation Ltd. Vs. Saw Pipes Ltd.3*
d. Waidhan Engineering & Industries (P) Ltd vs. the Board Of Trustees for port of Kolkata
e. Sleepwell Industries Ltd. Vs. Bank of Baroda CS.No.196 of 2011

HEAD NOTE

Foreign awards deemed "Decree"- presupposes enforceable - Court's to satisfy u/s 48 - Executing Court considering application barred by *res judicata*, without any compunction petitioned u/s 10 IBC - irrespective of any Indian court orders, on peculiar facts, Calcutta HC Registrar, after RBI permission encash FDs, remit and file compliance report. {paras 8,10,11,13,14,19}

SLP's dismissed with exemplary costs

SYNOPSIS

questions in both petitions are overlapping, answered together - contracts for sale of Non Basmati Parboiled Rice, Thailand origin meant for Bangladesh - Port of loading quantity was final - governed by Arbitration in London - respondent invoked inferior quality and non-release of payment are subject matter of arbitration dispute - petitioner not oppose, raised objection orally - court to satisfy foreign award was enforceable and record it - S.48 deemed decree as also foreign awards - review application ploy to reopen case - High Court, Executing Court was once again called to consider objections on enforceability - not be countenanced in view of the limited jurisdiction u/s 48 - *Shri Lal Mahal Ltd. Vs. Progetto Grano SPA1, Renusagar*

Power Company Ltd. Vs. General Electric Co.2, and *Oil & Natural Gas Corporation Ltd. Vs. Saw Pipes Ltd.3* - failed to participate in arbitration despite opportunity – AT jurisdiction to decide - petitioner not alleged fraud or bias against AT - rejected petitioner's objections on enforceability, devoid of merits - once again approached this Court reiterated HC taken objections - Executing Court considering application u/s 48 has acted as a First Court of appeal and assumed powers under Order 41 Rule 33 of CPC and sustained award by supplying new reasons and facts - petitioner application not maintainable as *res judicata* - attempt to overreach - after the interim order respondent permitted to withdraw, petitioner changed its name, registered office - without any compunction, proceeded to file a petition u/s 10 IBC – appealed to invoke moratorium against further release money to respondent - same not disclosed, while obligated under law - petitioner has allowed the said awards to attain finality having failed to file such appeal - argument of fraud not brought to AT notice by respondent – respondent would contend that such direction is necessary in the peculiar facts of present case and to obviate any complication due to moratorium, as the petitioner has invoked proceedings under IBC - argument in desperation only to protract executing foreign award on untenable grounds - subject foreign awards deemed decree, presupposes enforceable – S.48 not envisage piecemeal consideration- enforceability scope of interference consciously constricted by legislature - enforceability S.48 considered every aspect - limited scope for interference - AT considered all aspects - even if error, correction by appeal under English Law - SLP's dismissed with exemplary costs - irrespective of any order passed in India, peculiar facts made specific order Registrar (OS), Calcutta HC forthwith encash FDs lying in execution case after RBI permission - remit including interest accrued in US Dollars to respondent in 8 weeks from today and file compliance report.

<u>Abbreviations</u>

AT - Arbitral Tribunal

FD- Fisxed Deposits

HC – High Court

IBC- Insolvency and Bankruptcy Code, 2016

RBI- Reserve Bank of India

SLP- special leave petition

D.O.J: 20.02.2019

NBR (2019) (02) (08) (01)

IN THE SUPREME COURT OF INDIA
CIVIL ORIGINAL / INHERENT JURISDICTION
WRIT PETITION (CIVIL) NO. 845 OF 2018
RELIANCE COMMUNICATION LIMITED & ORS .....PETITIONERS
VERSUS
STATE BANK OF INDIA & ORS ..... RESPONDENTS
WITH
CONTEMPT PETN. (C) NO. 1838 OF 2018 IN W.P. (C) NO. 845 OF 2018
CONTEMPT PETN. (C) NO. 55 OF 2019 IN W.P. (C) NO. 845 OF 2018
AND
CONTEMPT PETN. (C) NO. 185 OF 2019 IN W.P. (C) NO. 845 OF 2018

R.F. Nariman & Vineet Saran ....JJ.

<u>Cases referred:</u>

a. *Attorney-General v. British Broadcasting Corporation, [1980] 3 All ER 161*

b. *Attorney-General v. Leveller Magazine Ltd. and Ors., [1979] 1 All ER 745*

c. *Lakshman Prasad Agarwal v. Syed Mohammad Kareem, 2009 (6) SCALE 413*

d. *Rosnan Sam Boyce v. B.R. Cotton Mills Ltd., (1990) 2 SCC 636*

e. *Babu Ram Gupta v. Sudhir Bhasin, (1980) 3 SCC 47*

f. *Ashok Paper Kamgar Union v. Dharam Godha, (2003) 11 SCC 1*

g. *Dinesh Kumar Gupta v. United India Insurance Co. Ltd., (2010) 12 SCC 770*

h. *Ahmed Ali v. Supdt., District Jail [1987 Cri LJ 1845 (Gau)] and B.K. Kar v. High Court of Orissa [AIR 1961 SC 1367 : (1961) 2 Cri LJ 438]*

a. *State of Bihar v. Rani Sonabati Kumari [AIR 1954 Pat 513] and N. Baksi v. O.K. Ghosh [AIR 1957 Pat 528]*

j. *Supreme Court Bar Assn. v. Union of India, (1998) 4 SCC 409*

k. *Chhaganbhai Norsinbhai v. Soni Chandubhai Gordhanbhai, (1976) 2 SCC 951*

ax. *Patel Rajnikant Dhulabhai v. Patel Chandrakant Dhulabhai, (2008) 14 SCC 561*

all. *Noorali Babul Thanewala v. K.M.M. Shetty, (1990) 1 SCC 259*

<u>HEAD NOTE</u>

Ericsson contempt against 3 ADAG Reliance companies and another against SBI, lead JLF - IBC invoked, IRP appointed, NCLAT stayed – now NCLAT Interim Order u/s 9 dt. 30.05.18 'key' - revived CIRP – Reliance undertakings turned down - to pay Ericsson in 1 week and remove contempt in 4 weeks, in default Chairmen 3 months jail and INR 1 crore fine to each Company - In default,1 more month's jail [paras 1,2,13,21,24] CONTEMPT

PETITIONS DISPOSED

SYNOPSIS

Ericsson contempt petitions against 3 ADAG Reliance companies - Ericsson provided operation, maintenance, and management for Reliance network - 3 notices under IBC - u/s 9 IBC too applied as operational creditor - NCLT admitted, appointed 3 IRP - NCLAT stayed recorded matter settled for Rs.550 crore be paid in 120 days - 'Undertakings' serious bone of contention – first contempt petition by Ericsson - reliance seek extension of time, heard, till 15.12.2018 pay with 12% p.a - extension sought for DoT's NOC to sell other spectrum – declined, dismissed as withdrawn - Ericsson moved SC to effectuate settlement – Reliance wrote to stock exchanges not resist CIRP, hitherto stayed – 3rdcontempt petition notice against SBI, headed JLF of 46 financial creditors - mischievously undertakings now filed contrary to SC order dated 03.08.2018 - first contempt petition, no *bona fide* efforts to pay-contrary to letter dt. 21.1.19 be paid in 10 days - DoT insisted on guidelines, not give NOC - CIRP now go forward - SBI argued CIRP nothing to do with Ericsson transaction - Everything turns on 30.05.2018 NCLAT Order u/s 9 of IBC – impugned AA orders 15.5.18 and 18.5.18, CIRP stay - JLF to sell Reliance assets – Reliance pay Rs. 550 Crores in 120 days by 30.9.18 – non payment, then, appeal(s) dismiss Operational Creditor pay back to Reliance - last opportunity be paid before 15.12.2018 with 12% p.a. interest - revive I.A. for contempt, if not paid - both undertakings and NCLAT order militate any linkage - Ericsson protest no further extension - spectrum sale to Reliance Jio not fructify - new facts, Reliance letter dated 21.01.19 willing to pay if contempt petitions and arbitration withdrawn- Ericsson replied, instead about-turn by Reliance - Ericsson in lurch – revive CIRP - Attorney-General v. British Broadcasting Corporation, [1980] 3 All ER 161 - protect justice administration - contempt disappear from vocabulary - in Attorney-General v. Leveller Magazine Ltd. and Ors., [1979] 1 All ER 745 justice itself flouted - remember letter and spirit of order inLakshman Prasad Agarwal v. Syed Mohammad Kareem, 2009 (6) SCALE 413 - In Rosnan Sam Boyce v. B.R. Cotton Mills Ltd., (1990) 2 SCC 636 undertaking false to its knowledge – proceedings quasi criminal - law of contempt strictly interpreted - fail to see how Reliance not guilty of contempt - reject unconditional apology - cavalier attitude - Reliance relied on Babu Ram Gupta v. Sudhir Bhasin, (1980) 3 SCC 47, no application - In Ashok Paper Kamgar Union v. Dharam Godha, (2003) 11 SCC 1 - not require any extraordinary effort nor dependent on third party, not apply – beginning itself deliberate misstatement - In

Dinesh Kumar Gupta v. United India Insurance Co. Ltd., (2010) 12 SCC 770, not correct to overlook S.2(*b*) - no civil contempt if disobeyed order itself provides scope - not correct infer misapprehension acted - *Ahmed Ali v. Supdt., District Jail* [1987 Cri LJ 1845 (Gau)] and *B.K. Kar v. High Court of Orissa* [AIR 1961 SC 1367 : (1961) 2 Cri LJ 438] unintentional disobedience not enough; further in *State of Bihar v. Rani Sonabati Kumari* [AIR 1954 Pat 513] and *N. Baksi v. O.K. Ghosh* [AIR 1957 Pat 528] not render punishment no contempt against SBI, Chairman - Ericsson and JLF assets sale independent - Supreme Court Bar Assn. v. Union of India, (1998) 4 SCC 409 object both curative and corrective - disobey undertaking apart from punishing police force recover possession - In Chhaganbhai Norsinbhai v. Soni Chandubhai Gordhanbhai, (1976) 2 SCC 951, deliberate flouted, except convicted - in Patel Rajnikant Dhulabhai v. Patel Chandrakant Dhulabhai, (2008) 14 SCC 561, apology are tactful moves, award jail - in Noorali Babul Thanewala v. K.M.M. Shetty, (1990) 1 SCC 259 injunction breach tantamount – settled, civil proceeding undertaking breach is contempt, jail or fine or all - INR 453 crore be paid to Ericsson and deposit INR 118 crore Court Registry – in turn, Registry pay to Ericsson in 1 week - Reliance purge the contempt in 4 weeks - default, Chairmen given undertakings jail 3 months and INR 1 crore fine to each Company, paid to Registry in 4 weeks for SC Legal Services Committee - In default,1 more month's jail. Contempt petitions disposed.

———

DOJ: 27.02.2019

NBR (2019) (2) (3) (1)

IN THE SUPREME COURT OF INDIA

CIVIL APPELLATE JURISDICTION

CIVIL APPEAL NO.5043 OF 2009

SHRI RAM MANDIR INDORE .... Appellant

VERSUS

STATE OF MADHYA PRADESH AND OTHERS .... Respondents

R. Banumathi and R. Subhash Reddy, JJ.

CASES CITED

v. State of Uttarakhand and another v. Mandir Sri Laxman Sidh Maharaj (2017) 9 SCC 579 [para 12]

v. Goswami Shri Mahalaxmi Vahuji v. Ranchhoddas Kalidas and others (1969) 2 SCC 853 [para 14]

v. Tilkayat Shri Govindlalji Maharaj Etc. v. State of Rajasthan and others [1964] 1 SCR 561 [para 14]

v. Sadashiv Giri and others v. Commissioner, Ujjain and others 1985 RN 371 [para 23]

HEAD NOTE

No substantial question of law - Mandir title in Deity is 'Public' on evidence - pujari's estopped to deny Government control, auction, while Collector as Manager without notice illegal - not challenged land mutated as Pujari's, never as Inamdar - Mandir established by Naga Babas, no household, while Pujari's broke tradition, no blood relation - no evidence restrict public. [paras 5, 6, 7, 8, 14, 17, 18, 25,]

Appeal dismissed

SYNOPSIS

Appeal dismissed - Plaintiff / Appellant argued State Government ['SG'] no right to interfere in Shri Ram Mandir's ['Temple'] management and control {'internal affairs'} – sought 'declaration' and 'permanent injunction' against auction, alleged not utilized for betterment.

Written Statement by SG stated pujari are its 'servant' - no inherent right to Temple's property - District Collector, Ujjain is its Manager – appellant took the temple land on lease.

Earlier, issues were framed by trial court - upon oral and documentary evidence, decreed as 'private' temple - no evidence adduced by SG to establish pujari appointment - permanent injunction granted - SG has no authority to auction without authority of law –

First appellate court allowed appeal, sets aside trial judgment – held, it public temple – title vests in the Deity - Collector rightly recorded as Manager - pujari is only to perform pooja-archana - plaintiff not adduced any evidence showing temple belonged to one particular family.

Second appeal to High Court upheld first appellate court findings – no substantial question of law, hence, dismissed second appeal - Collector, as Manager recorded without notice, hence, illegal.

Concurrent findings of High Court and the first appellate court are upon evidence adduced - warrant no interference.

Cause title misleading - Key question is whether Temple is public or not and is appellant/Mahant in-charge of its internal affairs - Hon'ble SC in following 3 cases held against pujari's plea –

- State of Uttarakhand and another v. Mandir Sri Laxman Sidh Maharaj (2017) 9 SCC 579, held necessary material pleadings - claimed his ownership over such a famous heritage temple and land surrounding – in absence of any pleadings in plaint that pujari built it, cannot claim as private temple.

- Goswami Shri Mahalaxmi Vahuji v. Ranchhoddas Kalidas and others (1969) 2 SCC 853 Supreme Court held origin, affairs managed, nature and extent of gifts received, rights exercised by devotees are relevant factors

- Tilkayat Shri Govindlalji Maharaj etc. v. State of Rajasthan and others [1964] 1 SCR 561 public participation in Darshan and daily acts of worship very important to determine temple's character.

Appellant not adduced evidence for restricted public participation in darshan - two different pujaris, no blood relationship under hindu succession – both performing pooja for two separate idols in same premises for generations and no outsider allowed - rightly rejected by first appellate court - no evidence temple belonged to one family - governed by tradition of Naga Babas of Guru-shishya relationship – not have any 'grihashtha' household life – later, HC rightly held Mandir is not 'private' temple. Pujari, Bajrang Das broke tradition – he is married person and householder - first appellate court has rightly held temple established by Naga Babas cannot be treated as a private - no interest of particular person - Even, his appointment as pujari was on application to SG - said order contains Khata numbers and extent of land and mutating as pujari - Pujaris were never Inamdars - Inam rights conferred on Temple, not on pujaris - appellant not challenged till suit filed - appellant taken Mandir lands on lease – never owned by pujaris in individual capacity, estopped from denying Government control - Temple is public on oral and documentary evidence - regard to First Appellate Court findings, High Court rightly held no substantial question of law in Second Appeal – Held, Temple is Public - agricultural land given to Deity, not to pujaris - impugned judgment not suffer any infirmity.

DOJ: 28.02.2019
NBR (2019) (02) (04) (01)
IN THE SUPREME COURT OF INDIA
CIVIL APPELLATE JURISDICTION

CIVIL APPEAL NO(S).11311 OF 2013
WITH
C.A. NO. 1824/2014, C.A. NO. 9798/2014, C.A. NO.9797/2014, C.A. NO. 9799/2014,
C.A. NO. 14728/2015, C.A. NO. 14730/2015, C.A. NO.14729/2015, C.A. NO. 33/2017, C.A. NO. 1009/2017,
C.A. NO. 2641/2017, C.A. NO. 6160/2018, C.A. NO. 9563/2018
ADJUDICATING OFFICER, SEBI ....APPELLANT(S)
VERSUS
BHAVESH PABARI ....RESPONDENT(S)

RANJAN GOGOI ..... CJI; DEEPAK GUPTA AND SANJIV KHANNA ..... JJ

CASES CITED

1. *Siddharth Chaturvedi Vs. Securities and Exchange Board of India [Para.2]*
2. *Securities and Exchange Board of India through its Chairman vs. Roofit Industries Limited [Para.2]*
3. *State of Bihar vs. Deokaran Nenshi & Ors [Para.13]*
4. *Union of India & Anr. Vs. Tarsem Singh [Para.13]*
5. *Bhavesh Pabari Vs. The Adjudicating Officer, SEBI 4 (2008) 8 SCC 648 C.A. No. 9797 of 2014 [Para.14]*
6. *M/s. Shree Radhe Vs. The Adjudicating Officer, SEBI C.A. No. 9798 of 2014 [Para.14]*
7. *Hemant Sheth Vs. The Adjudicating Officer, SEB C.A. No. 9799 of 2014 [Para.14]*
8. *Ankur Chaturvedi vs. SEBI C.A. No.11311 of 2013 and C.A. No.1824 of 2014 are also disposed of. C.A. No.14728/2015 [Para.25]*
9. *Jay Kishore Chaturvedi vs. Securities and Exchange Board of India C.A. No.14729/2019 [Para.25]*
10. *Siddharth Chaturvedi vs. Securities and Exchange Board of India) C.A. No.14730/2015 [Para.25]*
11. *Akshat Tandon and Others vs. Securities and Exchange Board of India C.A. No.33/2017 [Para.31]*
12. *Badri Vishal Tandon vs. Securities and Exchange Board of India C.A. No.9563/2018 [Para.31]*
13. *Magnum Equity Broking Ltd. Vs. Securities and Exchange Board of India C.A. No.1009/2017 [Para.39]*
14. *Securities and Exchange Board of India vs. Rakhi Trading (P) Ltd [Para.43]*
15. *Securities and Exchange Board of India vs. Kishore R. Ajmera [Para.43]*

16. *C.A. No.2641/2017 (M/s Quantum Global Securities & Leasing Company Ltd. vs. SEBI[Para.44]*
17. *Durga Prasad Yadav & Anr. vs. Securities and Exchange Board of India C.A. No.6160/2018 [Para.46]*

HEAD NOTE

Penalty – SEBI invaded 'Fundamental Rights' pleaded – offence nature 'penal'- for repetitive default u/s 15J the AO can exercise discretion upto Rs.1 Crore for matters u/s 15A to 15HA - jointly dealt two appeal with no reason to interfere - SEBI's SCN delayed over 8 years - SAT upheld AO orders u/s 15HA for no disclosure in purchase and sale – same individual trading in dual capacity, not denied – grandmother expired, disturbed, not inspire confidence – again, in second appeal SAT affirmed delay in disclosure - appellant assailed AO order - synchronized trades between family restricted to two scrip's - violated SEBA, not public funds mobilization - rejected leniency as part of other entities larger game plan [paras 4, 5, 7, 19, 23, 25, 31, 35, 36, 41, 46, 50]..... NO COSTS

SYNOPSIS

Does Section 15J of SEBA gives Adjudicating Officer ['AO'] discretion for penalty quantify ['A'] - these powers eclipse u/s 15A to 15HA ['B'] - SEBA object to protect investors and promote securities market – Section 15J refers to repetitive default where each wrong is separate cause - u/s 15A penalty not file return etc Rs.1 lakh; extend to Rs.1 lakh each day, maximum Rs.1 Crore ['C'] - u/s 15J AO to consider unfair advantage, repetitive default, etc - B to be read with A – under 15 J explanation, AO discretion under B adjudication while u/s 15A small technical defaults apply – power exercise with no loss to investors, no unfair advantage, while appellant pleads invades fundamental rights arbitrarily - Section 15A(a) amended not retrospective, extend to C.

Clauses (a), (b) and (c) of Section 15J ['D'] merely illustrative, not preclude AO penalty quantum in like circumstances - narrow view be indirect conflict with Section 15I(2) of SEBA on AO jurisdiction - above apart, circumstances enumerated in D no relevance – may never arise in case of contraventions say, Section 15A, 15B or 15C of SEBA - failure to furnish information, return, etc. not give rise to D, conditions not exhaustive - circumstances beyond D be taken note.

appeal from Securities Appellate Tribunal ['SAT'], Mumbai order on appeals impugning three separate AO orders u/s 15I - Impugned order passed by Tribunal confirms AO penalty of Rs.20 lakh each u/s 15HA of SEBA for violation SEBI (Prohibition of Fraudulent and Unfair Trade Practices relating to Securities Market) Regulations, 2003 ('PFUTP')- belonging to same individual trading in personal name and sole proprietor – inter-se transactions and transactions with connected persons - no leniency - SEBI filed cross appeals aggrieved by AO without reasons deleted penalty u/s 15A(a) - grandmother of proprietor expired in relevant period, disturbed mind at material time - not inspire confidence - lacks reasoning – on appearance, submitted part information - not considered by Tribunal – appellants, Promoters' cum Directors of Brij Laxmi Leasing and Finance Co. Ltd ['E'], Bombay Stock Exchange listed - appellants purchased shares of E failed disclosures under SEBI (Probation of Insider Trading) Regulations, 1992 ('PIT') – then sold which violate Model Code of Conduct under PIT Regulations – Tribunal affirmed penalties, rejecting contentions of harsh, no intention, not caused profits, inadvertent not mala fide - no good ground to interfere – jointly dealt two appeals - Bhawani Paper Mills Ltd. ('F').

FIRST APPEAL, aggrieved by Tribunal order against AO order imposing penalty for SAST violation was upheld – appellants, promoters of F holding 54% of its capital - U/s 15Z of SEBA, cannot go into proportionality and quantum of the penalty unless offensive, intolerable - very nature 'penal'- factual findings not denied - SEBI should have issued show cause notice ['SCN'] in time, 8 years delay contended, not raised before AO, not clear whether argued before Tribunal - reasonable time on nature of default, prejudice caused, third party rights etc - find no good ground and reason to interfere.

SECOND APPEAL- violation of Regulation 7(1A) read with Regulation 7(2) of SAST Regulations - Tribunal affirmed delay in disclosure required in 2 days of intimation of allotment of shares, as per Regulations 7(1A) and 7(2) of the SAST Regulations - appellant assailed AO order - appellate order observes synchronized trades create an artificial volume cause price fluctuations, misleading potential investors - case of the appellant not lead to an artificial price movement - tribunal rejected saying were between family members restricted to two scrips - in SEBIvs. *Rakhi Trading (P) Ltd* broker not be liable merely facilitated in absence of material suggest negligence and connivance - Test of preponderance of probability applies for the adjudication and determination of civil liability for violation - appellant violated Sections 12A of SEBA and Regulations 3,4 of PFUTP Regulations and Brokers Code of Conduct - appellant did not dispute findings - pleaded leniency – rejected part of larger game plan with other entities - 15HA penalty be upto Rs.25 cr or three times profit, whichever was higher, correct findings and unchallengeable – furnish information u/s 11AA of SEBA and SEBI (Collective Investment Schemes), Regulations, 1999 ('CIS') - inordinate delay, fresh summons u/s 11C(3), again no response - second summons no response – SCN part replied - SEBI email to appear, authorized representative appeared, not provided required documents – background, Madhya Pradesh High Court orders in 2010 for cheating by promising high returns - SEBI u/s 11C of SEBA, CBI and others liberty given for action.

No violation in public funds mobilization – contentions rejected as belated, afterthought and contradicted - no distinction as to documents within their possession and with police. AO rightly recorded non-compliance of summons hampered investigation, without justification- details withheld to delay SEBI investigation in contravention of CIS Regulations - No interfere in INR 1 Crore penalty Section 11C (3) under Section 15A(a) SEBA violate - Order dated 14.3.2016 subject Civil Appeals disposed - no cost.

———

DOJ: 28.02.2019
NBR 2019 (02) (06) (01)
IN THE SUPREME COURT OF INDIA
CIVIL APPELLATE / ORIGINAL JURISDICTION
<u>CIVIL APPEAL NO(s). 6221 OF 2011</u>
THE REGIONAL PROVIDENT FUND
COMMISSIONER (II) WEST BENGAL .... APPELANT (S)
VERSUS
VIVEKANANDA VIDYAMANDIR AND OTHERS ....
RESPONDENT(S)
WITH
<u>CIVIL APPEAL NO(s). 3965-3966 OF 2013</u>
SURYS ROSHNI LTD. .... APPEALLANT(S)
VERSUS
EMPLOYEES PROVIDENT FUND AND OTHERS ... RESPONDENT(S)
<u>CIVIL APPEAL NO(s). 3969-3970NOF 2013</u>
U-FLEX LTD. .... APPELLANT(S)
VERSUS
EMPLOYEES PROVIDENT FUND AND ANOTHER ....
RESPONDENT(S)
<u>CIVIL APPEAL NO(s). 3967-3968 OF 2013</u>

MONTAGE ENTERPRISES PVT. LTD. .... APPELLANT(S)
VERSUS
EMPLOYEES PROVIDENT FUND AND ANOTHER ....
RESPONDENT(S)
<u>TRANSFER CASE (C) NO(S). 19 OF 2019</u>
(ARISING OUT OF T.P (C) NO.1273 OF 2013)
THE MANAGEMENT OF SAINT- GOBAIN GLASS INDIA
LTD......PETITIONER(S)
VERSUS
THE REGIONAL PROVIDENT FUND COMMISSIONER, EMPLOYEES'
PROVIDENT FUND ORGANISATION ....RESPONDENT(S)

Arun Mishra and Navin Sinha .... J.J.

Cases referred

v. Municipal Academy of Higher Education vs. PF Commissioner, (2008) 5 SCC 428

v. Kichha Sugar Company Limited through General Manager vs. Tarai Chini Mill Majdoor Union, Uttarakhand, (2014) 4 SCC 37

v. Bridge and Roof Co. (India) Ltd. Vs. Union of India. (1963) 3 SCR 978

v. Muir Mills Co. Ltd., Kanpur Vs. Its workmen, AIR 1960 SC 985

<u>HEAD NOTE</u>

Basic Wages definition - Is PF to be deducted on Special Allowance(s) listed u/s 2(b)(ii) and s. 6 - respondent camouflaged the allowances - basic wages not defined - statute definition taken as dictionary meaning - universally paid to all included while specially paid not basic wages - u/s 6 PF contribution is on basic wages, DA, retaining allowance, whatever paid to permanent employees – DA is excluded u/s 2(b)(ii) but included u/s 6 – 2(b)(ii) excludes certain allowances being price of labor which must be earned. [paras 5,8,11,12]

Civil Appeal No. 6221 of 2011only allowed

<u>SYNOPSIS</u>

common question of law – u/s 2(b)(ii) and 6 for PF deduction computation does Spl.A fall in 'basic wages' – u/s 6 PF contribution on basic wages, DA, and retaining allowance - excludes incentive when direct nexus with extra output - whatever is payable to permanent employees included u/s 6 - retaining allowance in seasonal factories included – HRA, Overtime to some employees excluded - only emoluments earned in terms of employment qualify as basic wage and discretionary allowances not earned not covered - statute itself excludes certain allowance - exclusion of DA u/s 2(b)(ii) is exception, but included u/s 6 - attendance incentive not in terms of employment not fall in basic wage - transport/conveyance allowance, HRA, canteen allowance not included while conveyance allowance paid to all without proof, unsustainable - basic wage, would not ipso-facto take salary breakup for PF deductions when paid as special incentive to eligible workmen - when a worker produces beyond standard fall outside it - test is payment under the scheme must have a direct access and linkage - in Bridge & Roof (supra) 'basic wages' paid in cash - if no exceptions been no diffiulty in holding production bonus be included - 2(b)(ii) excludes certain allowances being price of labour, must be earned - whatever to permanent employees paid is included u/s 6 - overtime allowance not be earned by all - commission or any other similar allowance excluded - DA is exception, but corrected by included - Municipal Academy of Higher Education vs. PF Commissioner, (2008) 5 SCC 428, relying upon Bridge Roof's case observed (a) wage is universally necessarily and ordinarily paid to all are basic wages (b) Specially paid not basic wages (c) special incentive exclude - basic wage not defined - Kichha Sugar Company Limited through General Manager vs. Tarai Chini Mill Majdoor Union, Uttarakhand, (2014) 4 SCC 37, salary based on cost of living and used exclusive of additional payments - when not defined, statute definition take as dictionary meaning - those universally, necessarily and ordinarily paid to all are basic wage - no material not paid to all employees - allowances in question basic wage part - camouflaged to avoid PF deduction and contribution - appeals merit no interference, allowed - civil appeal no. 6221 of 2011 is allowed while rest and transfer case dismissed. Appeal is allowed.

———

DOJ: 15.03.2019
NBR 2019 (3) (5) (1)
IN THE SUPREME COURT OF INDIA
CIVIL APPELLATE JURISDICTION
CIVIL APPEAL NO.2424 OF 2019
(arising out of SLP(C) No.3551 of 2018)
S. SREESANTH ... APPELLANT(S)
VERSUS
BCCI & ORS ... RESPONDENT(S)

<u>Decided cases:</u>

v. *BCCI vs. Cricket Association of Bihar and others, (2015) 3 SCC 251*

v. *Writ Petition (C) No.318 of 2013 Sulaxsha Awasthi vs. Union of India*

v. *State of Andhra Pradesh vs. Chitra Venkata Rao, (1975) 2 SCC 557*

v. *State of A.P. v. S. Sree Rama Rao*

v. *Syed Yakoob v. K.S. Radhakrishnan*

v. *Union of India and others vs. P. Gunasekaran, (2015) 2 SCC 610*

v. *Central Industrial Security Force and others vs. Abrar Ali, (2017) 4 SCC 507*

v. *State Bank of Bikaner & Jaipur v. Nemi Chand Nalwaya*

v. *B.C. Chaturvedi v. Union of India,*

v. *Union of India v. G. Ganayutham,*

v. *Bank of India v. Degala Suryanarayana and High Court of Judicature at Bombay v. Shashikant S. Patil*

v. *Commissioner of Police, New Delhi vs. Narender Singh, (2006) 4 SCC 265*

v. *Kamaladevi Agarwal v. State of W.B., 2002 (1) SCC 555*

v. *Jagmohan Singh vs. The State of U.P., (1973) 1 SCC 20*

v. *Bachan Singh vs. State of Punjab, (1980) 2 SCC 684*

v. *Shailesh Jasvantbhai and another vs. State of Gujarat and others, (2006) 2 SCC 359*

v. *Gopal Singh vs. State of Uttarakhand, (2013) 7 SCC 545*

v. *Mukesh and another vs. State (NCT of Delhi)and others, (2017) 6 SCC 1*

ASHOK BHUSHAN AND K.M.JOSEPH ....JJ

HEAD NOTE

Life Ban set aside - BCCI to revisit decision in 3 months hereof and future as per it - appellant did not question Disciplinary Committee's ['DC'] constitution, not violate Natural Justice principles, cannot challenge now - no legal impediment in Mr. Srinivasan, Ex-BCCI President participate in DC [Paras 60, 61]...PARTIES TO BEAR THEIR OWN COSTS

SYNOPSIS

Sports prominent place in one's life - promotes goodwill, friendship - International charter aims to develop- national institutions play major role by developing decentralized plan - IPL match in Mohali, Punjab - BCCI 'Society' under SRA banned appellant for life - DP suo moto registered crime case - appellant and Delhi bookies arrested - confessed under pressure - PR sufficient evidence - denied spot fixing - SR relied on audio conversation - tucked white towel, pleads superstitious, not in original reply - Rs.10 lakh to charity not accepted - bribe, no evidence - prayed natural justice principles breached - challenged DC constitution – jurisdiction, afterthought.

ISSUE NO.1: cannot ignore telephonic conversation - PR without statement in Police custody, not confronted – released, statement taken and SR submit - violate natural justice principles by DC.

ISSUE NOS. 2 AND 3: not open for SC, HC to substitute its own opinion - error of fact cannot be corrected, however grave - If enquiry made fairly on evidence, not interfere – earlier HC held no direct link, assuming had knowledge, 4 years suffered.

ISSUE NO.4: DC wrongly placed burden of proof upon appellant - alleged offence committed.

ISSUE NO.5: vast distinction in criminal trial and DC inquiry - guilty of criminal statutes offence, to prove charge beyond all reasonable doubt - SC judgment observations will not effect appeal pending for discharge.

ISSUE NO.6 - no legal impediment for Mr. Srinivasan, ex-BCCI President participate in DC proceedings.

ISSUE NOS.7, 8 AND 9 - disclose inside Information, etc - principle of just punishment is bedrock of sentencing, not be excessive - after criminal case discharge, no NOC, modify Ban by BCCI.

Conclusion: not questioned DC constitution, cannot challenge now – DC did not violate Natural Justice principles - not open to SC or HC to substitute their own opinion - no legal impediment in Mr. Srinivasan participate in DC - life ban set aside and BCCI to revisit its decision in 3 months - future in accordance with decision so taken - parties bear their own costs.

DOJ: 01.04.2019

NBR 2019 (04) (09) (01)

IN THE SUPREME COURT OF INDIA

CIVIL APPELLATE JURISDICTION

CIVIL APPEAL NOS. 3351-3352 / 2019

(ARISING OUT OF SLP (C) 8398-8399/2019, D. NO. 44809 OF 2018)

DR. D. J. DE SOUZA .... APPELLANT

VERSUS

MD, CPC DIAGNOSTICS PVT. LTD .... RESPONDENT

Dr. Dhananjaya Y. Chandrachud & Hemant Gupta) .... JJ

<u>cases referred:</u>

None

HEAD NOTE

No deficiency in service established – Before SC argued UPS be good, provided required item hooked up to UPS - no merit in appeal - brochure no commitment for pre-installation conditions - USA manufacturer e-mail found not override installation pre-conditions - no restrictive UTP or defect found by Consumer courts. ....APPEALS DISMISSED.

SYNOPSIS

NCDRC order 14.12.17 and on Review Petition on 04.10.18 - PO in response to quotation – remitted 50% instrument cost - not suitable advised to purchase 1KVA Online UPS - appellant is that he has got a confirmation from USA manufacturer is suitable but the respondent insisted - good provided that the instrument is the only item hooked up to the UPS - grievance no on-board laundry - instrument no use - sought payment with 9% interest and damages - District Forum dismissed complaint *inter alia* not placed order in support- no commitment from respondent either - appeal before State forum dismissed respondent has indulged in restrictive UTP not accepted - found order placed when respondent communicated their best offer - brochure mention of on-board cooling facility, but, no feature - dismissed appeal. NCDRC Revision unsuccessful - found no commitment and appellant failed to establish malfunctioning or manufacturing defect - continuous uninterrupted electricity supply necessary through Online UPS - fluctuation in electricity supply advised - Before SC argued UPS be good, provided required item hooked up to the UPS - no merit in appeal - pre-installation requisite clearly stipulate air-conditioned room plus 1KVA Online UPS plus Broadband - equipment will be provided with "i-track" remote facility at installation - brochure no commitment instrument supply nor could be any installation of the equipment without installation of 1KVA Online UPS - email from the manufacturer will not override the pre-conditions of installation in view of electricity supply conditions - no deficiency - find no error which warrant interference. Appeals Dismissed.

DOJ: 02.04.2019
NBR 2019 (04) (07) (02)
IN THE SUPREME COURT OF INDIA
CIVIL ORIGINAL/APPELLATE JURISDICTION
TRANSFERRED CASE (CIVIL) NO.66 OF 2018
IN
TRANSFER PETITION (CIVIL) NO.1399 OF 2018
DHARANI SUGARS AND CHEMICALS LTD. ... PETITIONER
VERSUS
UNION OF INDIA & ORS. ... RESPONDENTS
WITH

WRIT PETITION (CIVIL) NO.339 OF 2018
WRIT PETITION (CIVIL) NO.802 OF 2018
WRIT PETITION (CIVIL) NO.1086 OF 2018
WRIT PETITION (CIVIL) NO.1110 OF 2018
WRIT PETITION (CIVIL) NO.1124 OF 2018
WRIT PETITION (CIVIL) NO.1142 OF 2018
WRIT PETITION (CIVIL) NO.1138 OF 2018
WRIT PETITION (CIVIL) NO.1156 OF 2018
WRIT PETITION (CIVIL) NO.1153 OF 2018
WRIT PETITION (CIVIL) NO.1166 OF 2018
WRIT PETITION (CIVIL) NO.1206 OF 2018
WRIT PETITION (CIVIL) NO.1212 OF 2018
WRIT PETITION (CIVIL) NO.1236 OF 2018
WRIT PETITION (CIVIL) NO.1296 OF 2018
SLP(C) NO. 31421 OF 2018
WRIT PETITION (CIVIL) NO.1316 OF 2018
WRIT PETITION (CIVIL) NO.1308 OF 2018
WRIT PETITION (CIVIL) NO.1359 OF 2018
TRANSFERRED CASE (CIVIL) NO.65 OF 2018
IN
TRANSFER PETITION (CIVIL) NO. 1404 OF 2018
WRIT PETITION (CIVIL) NO.1363 OF 2018
WRIT PETITION (CIVIL) NO.1364 OF 2018
WRIT PETITION (CIVIL) NO.1374 OF 2018
TRANSFERRED CASE (CIVIL) NO.71 OF 2018
IN
TRANSFER PETITION (CIVIL) NO. 1283 OF 2018
TRANSFERRED CASE (CIVIL) NO.73 OF 2018
IN
TRANSFER PETITION (CIVIL) NO. 1285 OF 2018
TRANSFERRED CASE (CIVIL) NO.72 OF 2018
IN
TRANSFER PETITION (CIVIL) NO. 1284 OF 2018
TRANSFERRED CASE (CIVIL) NO.75 OF 2018
IN
TRANSFER PETITION (CIVIL) NO. 1287 OF 2018
TRANSFERRED CASE (CIVIL) NO.76 OF 2018
IN

TRANSFER PETITION (CIVIL) NO. 1288 OF 2018
TRANSFERRED CASE (CIVIL) NO.74 OF 2018
IN
TRANSFER PETITION (CIVIL) NO. 1286 OF 2018
TRANSFERRED CASE (CIVIL) NO.70 OF 2018
IN
TRANSFER PETITION (CIVIL) NO. 1403 OF 2018
TRANSFERRED CASE (CIVIL) NO.69 OF 2018
IN
TRANSFER PETITION (CIVIL) NO. 1402 OF 2018
TRANSFERRED CASE (CIVIL) NO.68 OF 2018
IN
TRANSFER PETITION (CIVIL) NO. 1401 OF 2018
TRANSFERRED CASE (CIVIL) NO.67 OF 2018
IN
TRANSFER PETITION (CIVIL) NO. 1400 OF 2018
WRIT PETITION (CIVIL) NO.1383 OF 2018
WRIT PETITION (CIVIL) NO.1402 OF 2018
WRIT PETITION (CIVIL) NO.1400 OF 2018
WRIT PETITION (CIVIL) NO.1391 OF 2018
WRIT PETITION (CIVIL) NO.1411 OF 2018
WRIT PETITION (CIVIL) NO.1410 OF 2018
WRIT PETITION (CIVIL) NO.1438 OF 2018
WRIT PETITION (CIVIL) NO.22 OF 2019
WRIT PETITION (CIVIL) NO.1502 OF 2018
WRIT PETITION (CIVIL) NO.8 OF 2019
WRIT PETITION (CIVIL) NO.9 OF 2019
WRIT PETITION (CIVIL) NO.14 OF 2019
WRIT PETITION (CIVIL) NO.36 OF 2019
WRIT PETITION (CIVIL) NO.50 OF 2019
WRIT PETITION (CIVIL) NO.81 OF 2019
WRIT PETITION (CIVIL) NO.117 OF 2019
WRIT PETITION (CIVIL) NO.246 OF 2019
WRIT PETITION (CIVIL) NO.278 OF 2019

<u>Indian Cases referred</u>:-

1. Indian Banks' Association v. Devkala Consultancy Service, (2004) 11 SCC 1

2. Manohar Lal Sharma v. Principal Secretary and Ors., (2014) 9 SCC 516

3. Swiss Ribbons Pvt. Ltd. and Anr. v. Union of India and Ors., 2019 (2) SCALE 5,

4. Shayara Bano v. Union of India, (2017) 9 SCC 1

5. Independent Power Producers Association of India v. Union of India and Ors., Writ - C No. 18170 of 2018

6. Indian Express Newspapers (Bombay) (P) Ltd. v. Union of India [Indian Express Newspapers (Bombay) (P) Ltd. v. Union of India, (1985) 1 SCC 641 : 1985 SCC (Tax) 121

7. Harishankar Bagla v. State of M.P (1955) 1 SCR 380

8. Privy Council, vide Russell v. Queen [7 AC 829], Hodge v. Queen [9 AC 117]

9. Shannon v. Lower Mainland Dairy Products Board [1938 AC 708]

10. Delhi Laws Act case [1951 SCR 747]

11. Gwalior Rayon Silk Mfg. (Wvg.) Co. Ltd. v. The Assistant Commissioner of Sales Tax and Ors.

12. Devi Das Gopal Krishnan v. State of Punjab [AIR 1967 SC 1895 : (1967) 3 SCJ 557 : (1967) 20 STC 430

13. The Delhi Laws Act, 1912. [AIR 1951 SC 332: 1951 SCR 747 : 1951 SCR 527

14. Municipal Corporation of Delhi v. Birla Mills.

15. Harishankar Bagla v. State of Madhya Pradesh [AIR 1954 SC 465 : (1955) 1 SCR 380: 1954 Cri LJ 1322

16. Senior Electric Inspector v. Laxminarayan Chopra, (1962) 3 SCR 146

17. Central Bank of India v. Ravindra, (2002) 1 SCC 367

18. Sudhir Shantilal Mehta v. Central Bureau of Investigation, (2009) 8 SCC 1

19. ICICI Bank Ltd. v. APS Star Industries Ltd., (2010) 10 SCC 1

20. State of U.P. v. Singhara Singh, (1964) 4 SCR 485

21. Utkal Contractors & Joinery (P) Ltd. v. State of Orissa, (1987) 3 SCC 279

22. Bharat Sanchar Nigam Ltd. v. Telecom Regulatory Authority of India and Ors., (2014) 3 SCC 222

23. Union of India and Anr. v. Pfizer Ltd. and Ors., (2018) 2 SCC 39

24. Eera (through Dr. Manjula Krippendorf) v. State (NCT of Delhi) and Anr.(2017) 15 SCC 133

25. Arcelor Mittal India (P) Ltd. v. Satish Kumar Gupta (2019) 2 SCC 1

26. Asian Resurfacing of Road Agency (P) Ltd. v. Central Bureau of Investigation (2018) 16 SCC 299

27. Macquarie Bank Ltd. v. Shilpi Cable Technologies Ltd., (2018) 2 SCC 674

28. State (NCT of Delhi) v. Brijesh Singh (2017) 10 SCC 779

29. J.K. Cotton Spinning & Weaving Mills Co. Ltd. v. State of U.P., (1961) 3 SCR 185

30. Commercial Tax Officer, Rajasthan v. Binani Cements Ltd. and Anr., (2014) 8 SCC 319

31. Maru Ram and Ors. v. Union of India and Ors., (1981) 1 SCC 107

R.F. NARIMAN AND VINEET SARAN ....JJ

HEAD NOTE

RBI Circular dt.12.02.18 on stressed assets resolution bone of contention - government confined to S. 35AA and 35AB of BKRA and CG circular 05.05.17 - u/s 35AA IBC application, without CG authorization no power to RBI - S.35AB stressed assets resolution de hors IBC, exercised separately from S. 35AA - specific stressed assets cases RBI to intervene - all cases u/s 7 IBC declared non est. - question constitutional validity failed

DISPOSED ACCORDINGLY

SYNOPSIS

Questioned Constitutional validity of S.35AA and 35AB of BKRA - RBI Circular dt.12.02.18 on stressed assets resolution bone of contention – restructuring, 100% lenders concurrence - picking defaults INR 2000 crore and above is fully implemented before 195 days from reference or default, lenders file applications as financial creditors under IBC, lender whose stake is only 1% can stall RP *de hors IBC* make circular arbitrary and violate of Article 14 of Constitution - Relevant provisions BKRA and RBI Act and IC were *ultra virus* - Indian Banks' Association v. Devkala Consultancy Service, (2004) 11 SCC 1 S. 35A– interestingly, important sectors facing problem such as Power where Electricity Act is complete code for private sector with tariff fixed by ERC - relied heavily upon PSC report - 34 stressed projects debt exposure of INR 1,74,468 crore and NPA INR 34,044 crores due to Government policy changes, coal mines cancelled in Manohar Lal Sharma v. Principal Secretary and Ors., (2014) 9 SCC 516 - apply 180 day limit to all sectors is arbitrary - S. 35AA only file applications under IBC - S. 35AB stressed assets resolution *de hors IBC* -RBI Act and IBC intricately related - RBI Circular attempt to tell banks huge debts over INR 2000 crore given 6 months resolve or IBC move - relied on Swiss Ribbons Pvt. Ltd. and Anr. v. Union of India and Ors., 2019 (2) SCALE 5, Parliament leeway to deal economy – no arbitrariness, no excessive DOP – Sources of power u/s 21, 35A, 35AA and 35AB of BKRA - for NBFC u/s 45L of RBI Act - government confined to constitutional validity of S. 35AA and 35AB of BKRA and CG circular dated 05.05.2017 – CG authorisation u/s 35AA general - RBI PR dt. 13.06.2017 identified for IBC reference and revised framework on 12.02.18 - Ordinance and Amendment Act unconstitutional – in Swiss Ribbons (supra), economic legislation view with great latitude – in Shayara Bano v. Union of India, (2017) 9 SCC 1 Article 14 may be arbitrary, none pointed out how - u/s 35A vast powers prevent affairs detrimental – no dearth of guidance in other sections - plea of constitutional validity fails - <u>ULTRA VIRUS</u>- argument on "ongoing" interpretation of statute - generally, statutes deemed "always speaking" – specific power S. 35AA, without CG authorisation, RBI no power in specific defaults - S.35AB exercised separately from S. 35AA which emphasize "default" - stressed assets directions other than IBC be in S. 35A read with S. 35AB specify authorities stressed assets resolution, *de hors IBC* - as IBC application, such advice redundant – one section grants general powers cannot be utilized, as opposed to another section of the same statute, specific powers - PN dt. 05.05.17 "specific" stressed assets RBI empower to intervene NPAs resolution in "specific" cases - RBI authorized by CG directions only "default" under Code - directions respect of debtors generally, would be *ultra virus* S. 35AA - IC applies to banking and non-banking institutions alike, as in JLF which jointly lend sums of money to debtors - difficult to segregate them, if it is *ultra virus* insofar as banks - all actions taken fall - all cases proceeded against u/s 7 IBC, declared non-est – IC is *ultra virus* S. 35AA of the BKRA - transferred cases and petitions are disposed of accordingly.

Abbreviations

BKRA- Banking Regulation Act, 1949
CG- Central Government
DOP – Delegation of Power
EA- Electricity Act, 2003
ERC – Electricity Regulatory Commission
GCA- General Clauses Act, 1897
IBC- Insolvency B Code
IC – Impugned Circular
IPP- Independent Power Producers
JLF – Joint Lenders Forum
NBFC - non banking financial company
NPA- Non Performing Assets
PPA - Power Purchase Agreements
PSC- Parliamentary Standing Committee
PN- Press Note
PR- Press Release
RBI - Reserve Bank of India
RP – Resolution Plan